A LOVE THE WEIGHT OF AN ANIMAL

ELIZABETH GIBSON

A LOVE THE WEIGHT
OF AN ANIMAL

CARMENTA

First published in the UK in 2025 by Carmenta,
an imprint of Confingo Publishing
249 Burton Road, Didsbury, Manchester M20 2WA
www.confingopublishing.uk

The moral right of Elizabeth Gibson to be identified as the author of this work has been asserted by them in accordance with the Copyright, Designs and Patents Act 1988

Cover image and illustrations by Michelle Freeman

Printed by TJ Books Limited

A CIP catalogue record for this book is available from the British Library

ISBN 978-1-7393745-9-4

2 4 6 8 10 9 7 5 3 1

To my mother, Shelagh, with love and thanks

Fuel

I swore I would write poems
for you to tear into like bread rolls,
in winter, huddled up beside your heater,
burrowing into your shell to find your snail heart
and there it is, pulling and easing at your pace.
Poems for breathing out with, on evenings after
crossing the expanse of the day and people and hiding,
to huddle here, on your own lakeshore, gather kindling
ready to feast and fill out your edges, warm-kilned vase
of all that you can be. Poems to help you touch again,
strum your strings, tap your drums, whisper, *love is back,*
this love the weight of an animal asleep in your lap
or of a bowl of butter, sugar, and cinnamon to lick from
or your sketching pen working to capture her cheekbones
or that moment with someone, realising, *yes, they are!*
They mention their partner, he or she or they,
or their queer football team or choir or knitters,
and it is like a side-smile or like their fingers tapping
against yours, a tiny sparkling pebble placed in your palm.
Poems like those I gulped down in bookshops at nineteen
when I was rocky and jostled. Those poems rooted me
so that I could grow into rosebay and thistles and cowslips.
Breathe. Know that it is real, what we are. Never doubt it.

CONTENTS

Fuel	7
to be very warm and very cold together	11
Tintwistle	13
Self-portrait, without cat	14
Miracles you still find	15
The goose at the end of the world	16
To write without fear	17
Crocuses, etc.	18
First walk with the birdsong detector	19
Raspberries	20
Balloons	21
Three cygnets	22
Worms die	23
My period started at Strawberry Field	24
When I do bleed…	25
Could this be how to love?	26
Listing the fox	27
so many nerve endings, so many shades of green	29
June is a mouth	31
Finding joy in an underground supermarket	32
Jam the Mouse	34
Queer hiking in Anne Lister country	35
The squirrel and fainting	36
Athletes do it, don't they?	37
If I ever faint in front of you…	38
Devouring	39
Stretched with gulped sky	40
Cor marant	41
What I would pray, if I could manage prayer	42
Alert	43
After the heat	44

all big things start somewhere, and now, here we are	45
things we might never do in the night	47
Little ringed plover	48
Rest as radical	50
Strum	51
belly as dirty/sacred word	52
Hilbre Island	53
The fossil record for starfish	54
They have put an oxygen mask on the seagull	55
The fly house	56
Chocolate for dying dogs	57
Two swans	58
Arrival	61
Acknowledgements	63

to be very warm
and very cold together

Tintwistle
The Peak District

I know now that snow crystals are like glassy white grains of rice.
Tintwistle is the prettiest name of a place we have hiked from,
and the competition is strong: Winter Hill, Silverdale, Snake Pass,
Kinder Scout. But *Tintwistle* sits at the top of your mouth,

so nearly *tin whistle*, and I want to play mine here some day
for the dusty fell pony in its blanket, edible in its sugared-ness,
the treacly hilltops, ice roads. I have never seen real ice roads,
and here they are, shiny as teeth. The dogs pick and place tiny feet.

My very first teacher was Mrs Entwistle. I remember loving her.
My family used to go to Oswaldtwistle Mill sweet factory
so I could collect cinder toffee like fool's gold, smell pear drops.
Tintwistle is the silver version, with a blueish glow, a rare song.

There is a multitude of geese on the reservoir – such round silhouettes
– and a sprawl of kayaks roll and squeak against the ice edge.
Although I own a golden tin whistle, I can only see the word as silver,
the *i* a lighter note at the roof of my mouth-cave: tin, twistle,

winter, hymns, whisper, the mystery in glimpsing our finish,
which is also the beginning, where there is a firepit outside an inn.
Imagine coming here just to be very warm and very cold together.
Somewhere, the brown-sugar pony waits for her person, for mints.

Self-portrait, without cat

You spotted her! The fluff of tail leaving the frame.
What? Oh, no, the cat doesn't signify anything. She just meandered in
and was swiftly and appropriately removed.

Now, about the guitar. I bought it with my first-job Christmas bonus,
the most money I had ever spent at once. My sunburst.
Do you like my rock 'n' roll pose? I know, it's more of a sprawl.

Seeing someone female, or queer, or trans in full command of a guitar
is so goddamn powerful. I am unsure whether I am offering mine,
this wooden body, outwards, or pulling it back in defiance.

Yeah, I made the letters behind me: HAPPINESS, hung by thin thread.
I stencilled them onto rainbow paper and tenderly cut them out,
curving and sliding my hand, surprised at my smoothness.

I've flicked the more offensive dust and cereal clumps across the room,
out of frame. Focus – right – here. Yeah. that's great. Just me,
in T-shirt and jeans, with my guitar. This could be my legacy.

But what would *the cat mean?* You ask as we look at the picture.
Let's just say, there are times when life wobbles, when the heavy guitar,
the potential and sense of duty, hurts my back and shoulders.

The cat has weight, too – heat and ribs, whiskers – but it feels easier,
like something from the past... Hey, see that? A slice of the green
of her eyes, reflected in my brown. Fine. I give in to her meow.

Miracles you still find
Wigan

There have been three lemons in a line
        on the kitchen table for as long
                as I've been here this time.

    No explanation, but acknowledgement:
    I need a pen, I wail.
    There are some by the lemons, Mam says.
    I slump before the lemons, stretch for their verb –
    they don't rest, or perch, or sit.
        There has to be a name for the constant tilt,
            the sense that they will topple, each one so round
            with the tiniest portion
                of its being
                touching
            the table's wood.

        One lemon is pointing diagonally upwards.
                Curious, I lift it
    and see that it is supported by a clothes peg,
    and I move the peg
                    and see the lemon fall
to join the others in being horizontal, though that fairy
still up there in my brain wants to believe
    that it somehow managed
        to be diagonal on its own,
        a planet on its axis,
           one of those miracles
you still find,
        like flowers turning to the sun
                or bees dancing memories.

        I have had four hours of sleep.
        I couldn't breathe after sobbing,
            so I lay and read my book.
        Now, my salty tissues are banking up
            against the lemons, so I move them,
        wonder when the time will come
                for cake or tartlets,
the grating of skins, the raw belly clutched in a palm
like a pig's heart, fitting satisfyingly, being pressed hard-hard-hard
        until it is completely empty,
      its remains scooped up and held under a nose
        to – gasp – in.

The goose at the end of the world
Ancoats, Manchester

A belligerent goose has remembered that the towpath
belongs to him, and he becomes wider and wider,

> a *hisss* of steam as he inflates. On days when I cry
> about not knowing what friends are or whether

I have them, the post-blue dusk ripple of sky and canal
is empty and quiet, and I think of the playground

> at the end of the world, where there is no more hope
> or danger, no people, just your own clip-clopping

of footsteps, the goose an unexpected final encounter.
I make *pss-pss* noises, click my tongue without thinking

> – when I let go of the human part of me, life is easier.
> He retreats slowly: neck, then wings, then fan of tail.

I carefully sit by him, and we look up and down together.
He honks a sigh – an ending – and, after a moment, I echo it.

Written for the Ó Bhéal Five Words challenge

To write without fear

I didn't share the kestrel in the Gay Village
    years ago: my small red angel.
I won't share where deer run,
    where women run, where peregrines roam.
My window view and my walk home
    I paint with love, but I know and hate
        that there is a point beyond which
            I have to be vague.

    I won't tell you I love you. I won't mention names,

though, to my brain, word shapes are vital:
    the chewy green of her initial,
        the purple cut of yours.
I won't mention numbers, though they are also magic:
    ages, birthdays, the door numbers of my homes.
I won't give the animal
    of the year you were born,
        Rabbit or Tiger or Horse,

    how I see it in you, how it spars with the Dog in me.

Neither will I say your star sign, but one near,
    say, not Scorpio, but Cancer
        – but you are made of desert, not sea.
When we baked gingerbread for Pride,
    I could say flapjack, to disguise the memory,
        but... I can't do this neatly.
    I want to wrap you in power
        and poetry.

    Can I do that without hurting anyone? Show me, love.

Crocuses, etc.
Cheetham Hill and Ancoats, Manchester

Tonight, the wind is no longer pain-cold, full of grit,
but is instead a vast tongue, stirring to greet the spring,
curling and testing. It is still more cold than warm,
but it is a softer cold: organic, spongy, harmonious.
We smell woken soil, like air-dry clay, in the holly
for one step

                then it is gone, but you grin.
Yes, spring is scattering its first specks of warm,
of welcome, scouting, checking we are ready,
with our books to read in parks, loose denim jackets,
people to try to walk and talk with. The wind-tongue
shepherds us along, then presses us to pause for a pulse
by the canal, briefly tight as crocuses, saffron nerves
                                sparking red.
You pray for the purple to come. I pray to the viaduct,
its rust-dripped arches, and beyond, the great stacking
of what is still here: warehouses, pubs, woods.
Do you see us ahead? I ache for just one hug.
Maybe there can be nothing bigger. A hug is the pinnacle
of love and intimacy for me, as precious in its scarcity
as a few strands of spice rattling in their glass jar.
Maybe I should ask you, tease at this sliver of red
in a purple scarf and coat,

                        keep my heart petals open.

First walk with the birdsong detector
Leeds and Liverpool Canal, Wigan

Wigan canal-land swells from dusty-winter-empty
        to apparently sheltering siskins, redwings, a kingfisher
whose call I hear above me just as it is etched on the screen
        like a heartbeat. The synching up of it all feels strange,

like when your cat first brings a mouse in, and you realise
        that you must have had mice all along, gnawing away
at the fallen birdseed on the patio, you just never saw them
        until one was seized by the tail and dropped into your lap.

I wouldn't have thought this call could be a kingfisher,
        because it is not flowing fast and low over the blue water,
but steady in a bony tree on the other side of the towpath,
        where all is dry. I could have been hearing them for years.

I don't know how a siskin looks, but its name is pretty,
        like something I might call a child in some vague future.
But I can only go day by day, now. I escaped for four years,
        and at Christmas, it hit. I am resigned to being exhausted,

to my chest never not being uncomfortable, to being sad,
        but I think I'd always been sad, there just wasn't proof
like the smudges and blots of my sighs and coughs, caught
        on screen, as tangible as a mouse damp with spit and fear.

Raspberries
Hebden Bridge, West Yorkshire

And so,
after my cry
at the noise
in the world,
I sprawl out
to stare at pale
ceiling beams,
know that on the
walls are photos,
black and white, of
Hebden Bridge and
the hills and that one
will be Stoodley Pike
with its stone pylon in
whose heart chamber we
sheltered from the drizzle,
legs squashed against the
wall, and you held onto the
big collie's harness as she tried to steal from
my Tupperware, where my raspberries were
disintegrating into pools. You knew that losing
my food scared me and being in that small space
scared me. You held her firmly. The world was quiet.

Balloons

It looms, the arch of pastel balloons, from Wigan to Cheetham Hill.
I cannot escape their rubbery tautness, the impending bang and loss.

They settle in horseshoes at baby showers and christenings, so many,
glowing from the windows of Instagram. We are all reaching thirty.

The current trend is wild animals, lots of green. It is gender-neutral,
which is welcome, but I worry that the fondant tigers are judging me.

One night, my music group at the Irish Centre has to change rooms.
Our usual cubbyhole is floor-to-ceiling full of silver and blue balloons.

I ask to move – pleading, quiet – and we go next door, which is bigger.
I text those still to arrive, with balloon emojis to play down my fear.

We are in the Leinster Suite, I tell them. I remember Granny's house
in Wexford, where we would eat toast and jam and run in the garden.

I don't remember any balloons back then. Now, we blow whistles, sing,
strum, eat biscuits. No one expects any more of me than to make music.

Three cygnets
New Islington, Manchester

I know, really, you have no names, so I should let mine
fall away – those that I give you and those that people give me.
You are three-a-spring on our canals, then you disappear.

Could you be among the next parents, something I find
hard to wrap my mind around, or will you just... leave?
Take to the heavens, so free that you became a constellation,

bright as Cygnus over New Islington Green as I pace and cry?
They will ring your feet at some point. Will you protest
or keep your beak down, dark eyes fixed on chasms of wet?

Right now, you extend your neck, dabble the murky canal bed,
taste a piece of discarded fabric, then peck at the galaxy
of excrement that just fell and expanded from your parent:

matter of fact, no shame. Imagine, never feeling shame.
You get trapped on one side of the little wood bridge as it lowers,
your family drifting on the other. You don't bleat or flap.

You paddle up and down, up and down your side, never seeming
to consider hopping ashore and plodding round to join them.
The break is inevitable. But I am no swan. Teach me to let go.

Worms die

Central Manchester

Worms die on the pavement of St Peter's Square,
        two centuries ago St Peter's Field, where families protested
        and were charged by cavalry and crushed.

        These worms are mangled from inevitable boots
but tilt side to side, programmed to keep living until they can't.
        I try to see death as post-life, not not-life.

I search for any patch of earth, see only the squares
        at the feet of the giant foxglove trees, mesh tight over the soil.
        I wonder again if I could ever be happy

        if I left the city at last for countryside quiet,
or whether being an outsider and critical makes it all bearable.
If I had a house on a hill of fluffy grass,

        with nights of crickets and a river, would I crumble?
I can see myself curled up in a lap of wildflowers, sobbing,
        this should be it. I'm here. Now what?

In and out of scaffolding I bob with my umbrella,
        quick, practised, alone. Mam doesn't like me walking at night,
        but I am big and broad, and I just hope.

My period started at Strawberry Field
Woolton, Liverpool

I had never been, but here I was with my walking group, a spontaneous
extension of our Liverpool wander. Just one more stretch of leafy road
and mossy walls, to the new red gate and back, they said, but of course,
we ended up in the loo or garden, eating triangles of blondie in the café,
or cradling heart-shaped pebbles saying *hope* in the gift shop. I asked
nervously at the desk if the old gate still existed. They pointed the way.
I found its shaded-tree spot, almost a shrine, and touched it once, barely.

It was quiet and so very warm for winter, and I was always scared now
of what this warmth might mean later on. I headed to the loo and saw it:
the start, not strawberry yet, but strands of pink rhubarb in the tissue,
a promise, warning, gate opened to pain, dissociation, flushes of heat.
I rejoined the group. We were off at once. I dared to believe they waited,
noticed the absence of my awkward gait, my photography of tiny fungi,
and made sure that I wasn't left behind at Strawberry Field, burning up.

When I do bleed...

I am re-shocked by the power
that blood can gain
when it wants to burn
through cotton,
stay so dense, so itself,
a sturdy wax seal.
It is unashamedly live,
a wire, nothing safe
from its bite.

Between, many months
can pass with no evidence
that I still make blood,
and then, I do and am reset.
I see it and believe it.

And when it doesn't come,
I sit with myself, this vessel,
belly of meadowsweet
and moths and milky stars,
my pelvis a cathedral
to the empty that comprises
most of our universe,
the stillness allowing
existence.

Could this be how to love?

By sitting on my hands for warmth? I feel damp, and find them gullied
with red – no, coral. I have bled through pad, pants, pyjama bottoms.
By rummaging through every last cereal box, eating every single piece
of chocolate? The noise is a shock, scratchy and painful on my ears.
Being typical – like a moon – does appeal. The nurse said five weeks
is fine, but these days, I am hurtling like a meteorite into smaller orbits.

By forgoing my daily walk? It is bucketing down. I eat the remaining
cereal, gulp down granola lumps and milk. It feels like completion.
I didn't know that I could lose this much blood so rapidly and softly,
like I forgot that I could feel this peaceful and tender within my body.
It usually declares, *yes, you must go and march along frozen canals!*
It seems, for once, to give itself up: *yes, I will rest in your – our – lap.*

See that you feed me, keep me cosy – this is nice, isn't it? Intimacy.
We should try it more. Let it all go, become just warm lamp and pillows,
the rain clattering outside. Hold this sore person, this belly and back,
soothe the burning and wanting. Stroke this head like it is a little rabbit,
indulge in every sweet dot of chocolate, placed perfectly in the centre
of our tongue, and then warm your cold hands in these coral waters.

Listing the fox
North Manchester

Fox:
flutter of four limbs, across the road up our hill, no way
to tell it is fox, except what else would flicker like this
from dregs of cut forest to long-empty mills?

                                                                    Fox!
            Oh, the pluck you have, dancing openly across tarmac,
            human terrain, recalling the misspent days of my youth
                  engrossed in a browser game playing as a loner

fox;
you would chase bunnies, and try not to run out of energy
and keel over, or be eaten by a bear. Squatting to drink
from lakes of pixel-blue. No people anywhere.

                                                              Fox?
            Will I ever again make my home outside of a high-rise?
            I have a taste for seeing over the hills, to the horizon,
                  the glow from the late trams, yellow – russet –

fox –
and the Impossible Bridge, so-called for leading nowhere,
but look at it: its grey-black brick, so cuboid and stout.
I hope they never manage to pull it down.

                                                   Fox...
            Can't we list it? List the bridge, the iron-thump of railway,
            the rosebay in the carpark whispering in the night breeze?
                  List the birds in the remaining trees, list you,

fox,
list my books, pillows, quilts – two, for the cold – list me
being here, document that this time was wildly, sweetly,
undeniably lived, put up a blue circle saying,

                                                    'Fox'
            and I may not have made it big, been someone to remember,
            but I loved existing. I will keep saying it, so they know
                  how happy I feel, how blessed, that I see you.

so many nerve endings,
so many shades of green

June is a mouth
North Manchester

Leaving the overgrown old quarry, I rediscover my lips through
gulps of cold water, then sharp air clinging to the water drops,
to so many nerve endings, so many shades of green
I had never noticed, strangely glowing in grey light,
clutches of round trees, triangle trees, stretchy trees,
the thistles now covered in black spiky caterpillars.
I take a blurry picture for you of a new spiky friend.
You used to keep them in jamjars. I dream you here,
curling up caterpillars on your tongue. All those feet:
the front hooked ones that carefully pick and hold
and then the stubbier ones with the swimming walk.
My friend stings my ring finger. I did see it coming.
I bite to ease the poison, saliva warm, teeth marking
deeper than I thought, pink and loving and wet.

Finding joy in an underground supermarket

On the way towards home, the street loud,
                after a hike through hills or a day of screens,
the night clicks in, and you duck inside.
                      There is always relief in *sliiiding* down
on the escalator. Sometimes, the underground bit
                      is like a whole other world
– you can't go back up after going down,
                      and that can require planning, in a way
that makes things feel a little bit more adventurous
                      for a non-shopper like me.
Well – I shop, but I have never been gifted at it,
                never been able to float my way around the place
                deftly acquiring what I need.
But down here, it is cool – or it seems it.
                Maybe that is how our brains expect it to be,
                  like a cave, below the sun's reach.
There are so many yoghurts,
                their curves bringing calm, choice, sweetness.
There is the music, often 80s and synthy,
                and something primal in your blood answers.
I always remember my visits well
              for their unique shapes and journeys.
I often come for baking ingredients:
        a mint plant in a pot, cinnamon, lavender honey.
           I fold myself in like an egg, cracked and loose.
            Sometimes, I dally in the little furrow under the stairs
           and think,   this space is shared but is still
           empty.
        Something about me is drawn to that.
    Only I will ever know it from here, this angle, this moment.
Life is loud these days, and hot, so hot
            and chemical and fast.
You need to slip below, sometimes.
                  Going down,
                    into this ordinary sacred space,
the walls seem to sing and the mustiness is just right,
                like a church hall long ago.
I catch myself in the tilted-down gaze
                of the security camera screen
            and am surprised
    at how okay I am with how I look, how I carry my solid self,

            how I cut my eyes back at my reflection
            as if to say, I am all yours,
               and I am all mine,
and I forget how good this feels
                    when I am living up in the air.

Jam the Mouse
Ashton Canal, Manchester

I hope I truly rescued you, didn't make life harder,
sliding you onto card torn from the Elastoplast box
in my backpack, plasters cascading into its depths.
Lifting you high, high into your sky, to the greenery
(very human greenery, a brief boxy hedge permitted
to sit between canal, towpath, bricks of new builds).
I slid you off your stretcher, and you shuddered
in your unsatisfactory green cave, and I moved on.

Or, I can tell it truly: I saw an oval-and-string mouse
dead but whole on the towpath, took pictures for Mam,
always desperate for her to know we have nature here,
even if only visible when something ends its movement.
Then   you rippled   with breath. She advised me
to find some card, any, to get you quickly to greenery,
that you probably had a fright from a seagull or dog.
I sent her another photo of you sheltered and shivering.

The tale became mine: I named you Jam after the event,
dreamed of so many mice named for spreads: Honey,
Butter, Marmite. I never learn that a door nudged ajar
doesn't always mean a deluge, a parade of toasted joy.
Next day, I did a minimal recce of the area and hedge,
with no sign of you. I had a gnawing feeling of doom.
I told myself, no, not-seeing is optimal, live mice move,
uncurl, scuttle under darkness to the next warm place.

I don't look back on the pictures though I expect to.
Jam, proof of a finding and a fleeting coexistence.
I was here, outside myself. Jam, a break from birds
and snails, that bit closer to people, us legged ones,
snuffling for company. I like to tell how I learnt to
lower myself so creatures could clamber up to me,
but I scooped you up, didn't I, Jam? You are a myth,
now, a symbol of all round mice, or of my rescuing.

Queer hiking in Anne Lister country
Halifax, West Yorkshire

Stalky wildflowers at waist height or maybe chest height
it feels irrelevant where my body is when everything is
in constant motion each hiker each thorny
branch carefully pulled back replaced *thrum*
like a guitar string each of us protecting the next
from being thwacked in the face from having it worse
than we did *dead rat! dead rat!* ripples down the line
so that we can look away if we want to if we like rats
but I find dead creatures interesting I can see Anne Lister
taking it home to dissect she was fascinated by science
by how we live moving as a pulse we displace blue acres
of sky the sun a golden band around the melting cake of us
my sinuses and nostrils throat and eyes grainy with pollen
imagine the red speckles in a swollen pink bell of foxglove
I have run out of water am reusing a grimy rag of tissue
so close to asking *someone hey could I pour from your bottle
into mine just a splash and do you have a tissue
new and flat maybe even folded up creamy origami*
but I endure endurance is something I am practised in
there are such enormous dandelions silver fuzzballs
I could crunch off a stem *blooow* say *look at the dandelion!*
we are always somewhere near the next dead rat the next frog
or the bumblebee curled in a tree root *don't step on the bee*
passed down until we reach the church in Halifax
stitched cushions in pews Anne is believed to be under here
no one knows exactly where I use the church bathroom
new sweet white tissue bathe my face give thanks for shelter
for my people who hold back thorns for me without hesitation.

The squirrel and fainting
On the way to Hope Mill, Ancoats, Manchester

I think the corpse is a bigger animal, try to work out which,
in that split second before seeing and knowing.
It is like how the moments before fainting, or after dreaming,
last much longer inside us than they do out,
and feel looser as to what can exist – I picture giant rat,
small badger, or a creature I have somehow never encountered.
But one step, then one more, and there it is: a grey squirrel,
still completely intact, tail and body equally long and lush,
tiny face fixed forever on the next challenge.
With that car outrun, is there now a fence to scale,
a birdfeeder to jiggle, a cat to dodge?
You can only live this way, otherwise
you would just stop, sit in your tree, never know.

I think of burial, the words replant and repot coming to mind.
The squirrel is a spring bulb, fossil fuel, a mass of minerals
and starry matter. It will give, as it fades, and the earth will drink.
They will become the same.
Then, at the theatre, I faint, thinking of the blood test
that I am expected to book, about invasion,
part of me coming to exist outside of myself in a red tube.
Flat on the floor, I stare at a ceiling unit like a square frog
stopped in time, mouth gaping. I am gently told,
why get so worried about something that isn't even booked yet?
I don't know how to live other than to keep moving.
When I stay still, I get so scared of dying. I am already
forgetting that squirrel. Somebody should remember.

Athletes do it, don't they?
Salford

They have blood drawn all the time. You will get used to it:
shuffling on the paper-towelled seat, searching the song
in your ears for a message: 'Coming Around Again'
last time, 'Angel Eyes' the time before, and before that

– you don't think you had your phone then, with music,
but you had your mother. The nurses are here, though, still,
and kind. You savour fruit pastilles, close your eyes,
feel your teeth grind against the needle's scrape, float... away.

You are again grateful for the raised blue smudge of vein
that they can usually tap into with no tourniquet. All done,
they pinch you closed, and hold you like that for a while,
before smoothing on the plaster, the little sticker on an orange.

Over time, *athlete* has begun to ease into *atheist* in your mind,
and yet you are a believer, in the god of having your hand held
by a nurse, properly, as if you were their sibling or child,
the god of them saying to take your time, and letting you talk

about your upcoming smear test, saying they will hold
your hand then, too, if you need it. The god of not fainting,
but walking back across the river, texting your mother,
her knowing that you got through, this time, and you will again.

If I ever faint in front of you...

you will realise, I hope, how peaceful,
how gently ordinary it is for me.
The moments before
are the worst, all sick and dizzy,
but then after that, it is just like sleeping.
The exact moment is a mystery,

when I cross over to my mind
and its dreams. This world can be
so important, so real, my work there
so immediate, that I might well resist
getting up from the floor
when you ask me,

or did you catch me? Am I in your lap?
Either way, I am far, in some heather-y place,
and if I talk nonsense to you
as lucidly as day, I will probably
forget it all in minutes,
seconds, when I wake fully.

So, don't mind me.
Maybe this will bring us closer, maybe not,
but I just don't want you to be afraid.
Give me sugar – say, a vanilla wafer,
like my mother did, last time.
Hold onto my fingers, and I will be fine.

Devouring

My fingers reek of onions   ripe   primal
        bone-marrowish

and I am   back   back to dipping and diving
      back   inside my body   a squid full of ink

I had been living mainly off milky cereal
        then today I devoured a quiche   full of onion
               thick chalky crust   jaw working   teeth

    and then the *snap* of dark chocolate
           open fists of raspberries

I have missed feeding myself well
        this infatuation   acidic and heady

I am a sprawling   panting lion
               fangs trailing
                          strings of antelope jam

Stretched with gulped sky
Ancoats, Manchester

I used to think of parenthood, or something quietly formed over years,
silvery: trails of smoke, mountain streams, a map of my history.
But today's stretchmarks are fresh and sore, meaty ribbons of mauve

slicing my waist. There is such intimacy and defiance in it: in gaining
back some weight, filling out the ghost outline of my wider self.
How rare and sweet to be caught unexpectedly in the tall, thin mirror

of the accessible bathroom. I am not used to seeing my middle
during the day. This version of me usually resides in my flat at night,
tucked in a towel, hair damp, smelling of oranges. But even there,

I have not looked at my body in a long time. I guess it has been dark.
Here, now, in the harsh bathroom light, are new red marks
– new, or ancient, who knows? – and dark hairs, and my navel mole

that can fluctuate and scare me, and channels cut by my belt
into my quicksand gut, and the coin-shaped imprint of my jeans' stud.
I cover back up, piece by piece, then head outside, into the heat

to share space with dinosaurs of swans, with perfectly round geese,
with miles and miles of canals all swollen and stretched with gulped sky
and with feasts of lush green kelp to be gorged on by hungry fish.

Cor marant

New Islington, Manchester

I thought cormorant meant *heart of the sea,*
heart of a mariner, marauding heart,
like a pirate or merchant, a migrant, my ancestors
returning in bird form.

I searched, was told it meant *crow or raven of the sea.*
Mam likes crows and ravens, big and loud
and smart, making a ruckus in her garden.

But I can never get that *heart* out of my head.

That's what you are to me, really, my Cory-bird:
oil scooped from the seabed, the pulse of the Earth,
now clinging to a scant driftwood frame,
your dinosaur bones still showing through.

No one taught you to fly or plunge for fish.
It was just there in you, to rise from your underworld
into this open blue,

where you look odd and no one understands you,
except maybe my mother.

What I would pray,
if I could manage prayer
North Manchester

That this utopia of purple flowers and deer
and tall golden grasses can just stay forever,
that no one will touch the old shopping terrace,
egg-yolk sun pooling in its windows,
or our artificial ancient mound, where old men
bring bags of cans and mutter, *I'm just here
for a quiet moment, I come here sometimes,
you know*, as crickets and blackbirds call
in the blue twilight, the city a distant cutout
of skyscrapers, red dots flickering at their edges.

This place has been described as difficult,
but brimming with potential, as if they could stick
rods in and see sparks fly up, take the forms
of yet more unaffordable buildings, all concrete
and sheets of glass, tiny balconies and air con,
because it is so, so hot, will be even more so
when they have taken our trees: the hazels bent
into their round gate, the hawthorns pungent,
the birches catching the light at every last moment
before it hits the ground and is all gone.

Alert

On the road from Grasmere to Rydal, the Lake District

The morning when I naturally catch myself in a *She*
in place of a *He*, murmuring a love song, something is
settled, like when I found that I wasn't disturbed
by the badger, but leant in to check for movement as it lay by
the roadside, then sat in vigil with the
beautiful shell of it, traffic hymns whirring in my ear.
What I knew wasn't sadness or shame. Alert
to everything scurrying around, to growing as
dying, as an acceptance, each of us merely a
cloud of cells travelling on into the night, the heart a candle.

Golden shovel after Carola Luther's poem 'Architecture'

After the heat

New Islington, Manchester

It has stopped raining, and my cormorant has come back:
a neat brown clothes-peg clipped to the red wall
across the canal, over the bridge with its cobbles,
past the little cottage
with one light on.

And as I happily bump my way over towards Cory,
I accept, *yes, I can love an animal.*
Yes, I'm allowed to hurt if one day they are gone.

The goslings are getting big, and Yellow is back:
the smallest, always a week or so behind the rest.
I need to write a poem about Yellow.

Cinnabar grubs are officially here: skinny tiger-sausages,
vast tiger-sausages, curling or dangling from ragwort,
clinging on with iron-hook feet.

Lots of green weed in the water, after the heat.

The other week, I scooped an oval of mouse
from the towpath, deposited it under the boxy hedge.
It trembled, looking back at me.

I never used to see animals, but now that I have fallen
into myself, they seem to be everywhere.

They rise, as I relax, and we meet in the middle.

all big things start somewhere,
and now, here we are

things we might never do in the night

if I cannot fall open for you   a salt-snap oyster   let you lick me
if I cannot be a pantry of rich butter   jars of raspberry jam
nor a heart chamber   with three more waiting to slide open
nor a pass-the-parcel dropping coins   sweets   rubbery balloons
a red onion shedding its clothes   a pomegranate gushing rubies
an egg that caves at thumb-brushing   a sky to swallow firecrackers

then I will   hone my quickness on   the guitar of your belly
the tin whistle   of your cool golden limbs   chart your deep space
my mind lit by your meteors   catch your eyes and dark lashes
in candlelight   pray   learn the places where you ache and throb
sing to them   be tide to your island   soft-lapping your shore
deep in my nailbeds   the tang of your oyster   what I *can* give

Little ringed plover
North Manchester

I send Mam my birdsong results from fairyland (the old quarry
between the paint factory and tram line),
and she questions the little ringed plover, the spotted sandpiper,
the green-winged teal and the curlew.

She says if they are really here, they must be just passing, resting
on the way between waters.
I said, *that may be, but hey – in the city, we do have magical things*.
The trees heave with chirps and trills.

This wild swell of land is thrumming with grasshoppers and crickets,
dizzy-sweet with hawthorn,
peppered with foxes that I have reason to believe are shapeshifters,
home to slight, mighty deer.

I tell Mam, *I bet this place could offer sustenance to river birds, too.*
It could feed anything, surely,
there is so much, such riches. The moon in the dusk is a button, silver,
and I stay and stay and stay,

and why am I not better? I walk, and I drink water, and I talk to people.
Why can my heart, a plover, not stop
squeezing and shrinking like it is going to explode? Why do I float
up and up, out of my skeleton

to look down on myself? Why does adrenaline course through me,
keep me trembling and faint,
so I can never quite rest, and why do I find the word *love*r in *plo*ver
and still dare to see myself that way,

after accepting that I may never love like others do, with wet body
and complete understanding,
merging selves, sharing space and belongings? Why do I feel stranded
when I stop hearing plovers?

There is still the chorus of thrush, blackbird and robin: usual, solid,
what you would expect here.
The plover was a flash in the pan, a delicate passer-through, a comet.
I want to hold it tight and tell it

that it is so, so important, follow it to a valley with fresh running water
and, when it looks up, uncertainty
in yellow-and-black eyes, whisper, *hey, it is fine to feel sad, even here,*
however sweet the river at night.

Rest as radical

I tell myself   it is my new strategy   against   the perfectionism
    that is still a shard of glass at my core   surely I would disintegrate
without feeling   that I was always doing   something useful
    well   *hey*   *rest is useful*   *rest can change the world*
I can share it or hold it to myself   I am so piped-wired-cemented
    to everyone   a metropolis of life experiences   but rest as private
creates edges   my own shape   I can do everything as I please
    count my breathing   on my back in bed   window ajar
blackbird twirling words   *hey*   *pick a band*   *think of a song title*
    for every letter of the alphabet   *like you used to do*   *to get to sleep*
but why now?   I'm awake   I don't need to   *just because*

    tonight   how I relish the hours ahead   as I pull myself home
through the wet and echoey city   to my gate   up flights of stairs
    coat off   nooo   I forgot to buy loo roll   have to go back out
hey   *use baby wipes*   *they will feel nicer anyway*   *or Kleenex*
    little soft cuboids   but that is not good enough   not – proper
hey   *radical rest*   *remember?*   I bathe my face   warm water
    creamy soap   ease the stickiness from my eyes   check the lock
yes   my door is closed   I am in for the night   *now*   *let it all go*
    let the resting ahead fall over you   *in a bolt of shimmering*
purple fabric   *slide in*   *relax*   *it is time to accept* *your mission*
    fall into lazy bliss   *and maybe tonight*   *you will change history.*

Strum

I strum on my guitar first thing in the morning, sometimes at night.
It is tucked between my bookcase and the fold in the wall, reclining

by my bed, just how I long ago dreamt it. I touch two or three strings,
marvel at the massive voice that will answer, no amplifier or speaker,

just metal, echoey belly of wood and space. This curving hugeness,
burnished gold-brown, the circle at its heart, circles within circles,

the hips and shoulders of it. I am amazed at how I can be a constant
source of my own pleasure, propped up on my pillows, the bassline

of cars whirring up the hill outside. I can become reluctant to play,
thinking if I can't do it well, I don't deserve this sunburst miracle.

Maybe I don't care enough to practise fully, don't believe enough
to get on stage and be who I want to be: genderless, rugged, earnest.

Maybe I will never have that voice. But I have pieces of energy: bear
and spruce, salmon and wolf, the man and woman in me, the power

beyond it all. These guitar times, not quite awake or asleep, are holy.
I savour the taut metal against my fingers, rough as hair, and reach for

that note I heard in a folk song once, exactly when I needed to hear it.
Step in. Don't fear. Everything you needed was always right here.

belly as dirty/sacred word

oh how my palms find their way
to my belly always as I lie on my back in bed
feel hill of breath movement and that vein at the heart of it
tick-ticking leaving no doubt that this is the centre I would drift
off to space without but the other night nuzzling myself in my sheets
I ended on my front fingers tangling shorts and this was no taut drum
but handfuls of softness like milk why would I ever be repelled by this
I once wondered why I didn't flinch at a word brash and hard as a bell
yet the implied vastness and glut and audacity of B its swollen edges
saw me savour the silver sheen of something far away and forbidden
knowing I would one day plunge face and fingers into it knead
and need it like sourdough hear its bubbles and creaks kiss it
bite into it feed it butter and jam whisper I so love
your belly the word a piece of confetti

Hilbre Island
The Wirral, Merseyside

You tackle the hill with me, the latecomer,
    tell how the sea could take an isle any smaller.

        We reach the shore. You are shod, while I shudder
            at tiny shells in my bare soles, bask in kind water.

    Ahead, you warn me of the slime level per boulder,
        ask me to name birds. *Graylag geese?* I venture.

        You muse, *they do look goose-y – dapper.*
    We bounce over ridges of hard sand, and I wonder

how we can talk so deeply. My body remembers
    my feet learning cold, back when she held them under

        and I squealed. She said, *how will you ever be a hiker?*
Now, I stop you stepping in a milk-jelly creature,

    share how I never saw animals until I sat lower,
        and they rose to meet me, bats and foxes and deer.

        I try my first Wirral Rarebit when we rejoin the others.
            The mustard seeds pop, but it really is tender.

The fossil record for starfish

Lines in italics from the Wikipedia article, 'Starfish'

The fossil record for starfish is ancient,
        so is that why, when I learnt for sure that you were gay,
        I knew at once what I had to write about?
        You wrote songs about seas and islands and pirates,
        but they are not the ones that pull me open,
        feed me with orange and bronze, fishy muscle,
        make me go, yes, *yes!* This all makes so much sense,

dating back to the Ordovician around 450 million years ago,
        singing about queer love is the most obvious thing,
        your throat sandy, with the odd s*queak* like shell on shell,
        or a *catch* of breath, as you eased
        five limbs upwards to kiss the night sky.
        Poured like a praline chocolate, you push into
        every crack and corner. The echo of your rasp is so potent,

but it is rather sparse, as starfish tend to disintegrate after death.
        As a kid, I didn't get far in my epic novel about a dolphin
        adopted by starfish, learning to live like them.
        I was intrigued by them eating by pushing out their stomach
        through their mouth. My hungry, full, swollen part,
        so vulnerable for me, bared in order to taste ocean.

Only the ossicles and spines of the animal are likely to be preserved,
        I once had my back teeth suction-cleaned, which I hated,
        and my mother got me a beanie starfish. It wasn't cute,
        more of a small, misunderstood monster, eyes forlorn.
        I felt a love that we often don't have vocabulary for,

making remains hard to locate.
        I now thumb that love over the ridges of guitar strings,
        thrumming, something primordial, here since sea was sea.
        That unnameable, smelly, many-limbed magic.
        You were and are, we were and are. Remains is a verb, too.

They have put an oxygen
mask on the seagull

They are gently pulling a fishing line from its throat;
its eye is a wet-dark furrow in its yacht-smooth head.

The tiniest oxygen mask hovers before its beak:
do they have a stash of them tailor-made for seagulls?

For biggish birds? Or was it hastily crafted for this case?
The team are in scrubs, everything set out, such care

to not hurt it more, hoping it can soon resume its squawks,
its epic snatching of sandwiches from us, the unprepared.

A memory scratches at me, in which the seagull
doesn't make it. But I watch so many of these things,

I could be thinking of another patient, a swan or a hawk
– and yet the seagull hits different. It isn't cute at all.

Not a crowd-pleaser or endangered. It is just this life
that someone decided was worth a mask, worth saving.

The fly house

Étaín was turned into a fly
he built her a little fly house
with windows for her to leave
the pair travelled ancient Ireland
and did he feel self-conscious
I carry tired bees down streets
scoop moths from wet sink
guide snails to hedgerows
but also in that moment
the human world muted
I started asking everyone
maybe we should demand it
fell into Óengus' clothes
carried her everywhere
and return as she chose
mighty warrior and fly
but then why would he
furry buzz in my palms
to sweet dry windowsill
you do what you have to do
it really is only you and them
after learning of Étaín's story
can you imagine such love
I want a little fly house

Chocolate for dying dogs

I keep thinking of that viral photo of a bowl of truffles at a vet,
        the note saying to let your dog taste one before being put down.

It scares me, breaking the rules of life when I finally get them,
        because when you are entering the land of death, all rules vanish.

I don't know how to accept that actions won't have consequences,
        or none that matter, that there is a point crossed when you know

you can just feed your dog chocolate. An acceptance, a breaking,
        like pulling a bur from hair or fur, feeling the breeze through it,

gentle on a spirit and form now unsticky. I try to place myself there,
        licking a triangle of truffle from a trembling palm: this explosion

of unknowns, this taste and smell and feel, the first time it is safe
        being entirely because it is the last. You have to be almost there

to be handed this thing, feckless and otherworldly. The love in it,
        the mercy – I have felt them, however little I understand them.

Two swans
New Islington, Manchester

For once standing in shallow water, they are massive and exposed:
how could I have forgotten they are dinosaurs? I scan the marina,
houseboats, boardwalks. No hint of any dappled grey young.

I feel this ancient sense of comfort re-emerge: this can be okay.
As a duo, they are complete and contained, hewn from boiled egg
or cream, their bulging lower necks, mid-preen, fat as biceps.

When were they cygnets themselves? Three, four years ago, maybe,
before I discovered this place? Why does it bamboozle me so,
that these behemoths were tiny once, whether I witnessed it or not?

Not all small becomes big, not all nests stay warm. But all big things
start somewhere, and now, here we are. No babies in sight. Thriving.
They pluck at bodies like white heart-organs, fluffing the water.

They refuse to acknowledge me or shift for me to pass. Right now,
this patch of universe is filled with me and with swan. No one could
have predicted us millennia ago, but now, we will never be undone.

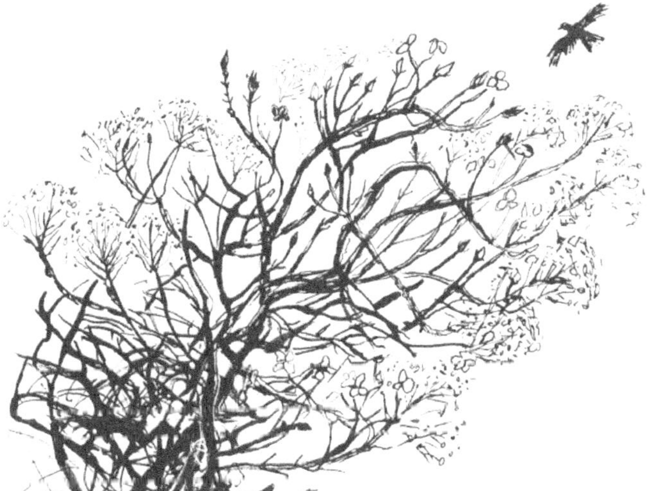

Arrival

Manchester

Once, a little fish swam across a wide, warm sea,
till it came upon an island, with a beehive, bright and pretty.
The fish so longed to stay here and know this honeyed city,
that it flopped out of the water and it dressed up as a bee.
It came to love the colours, the sweetness, and the buzzing,
and *knew* that it belonged here, for what it lacked in history
it made up with its wisdom from the ocean and her mystery,
and when it felt alone, in its mind the waves kept hushing.
Over time, the fish got braver, and let silver scales start shining,
to form a new mosaic with its black and golden fur,
and, daring to believe it could be true to both its worlds,
this new creature relaxed, spread its wings, and started climbing.
There was some doubt there, though, till that night when you told me:
But... you're a Mancunian! – so casually, and so free.

Acknowledgements

Writing an acknowledgements section for my first book was always a fantasy of mine. It feels surreal and wonderful for it to be happening.

I would like to thank:

- Confingo publisher Tim Shearer and Carmenta editor Tom England for offering me this opportunity and working with me to make it a reality. It is a joy to be the first poet chosen for Carmenta

- my illustrator, Michelle Freeman, for the perfect artwork and cover image for this collection. I always enjoy our collaborations and hope for many more

- the journals and presses that first published some of these poems: *Butcher's Dog*, *Dust Poetry*, Fly on the Wall, *fourteen poems*, Hidden Voice Publishing, *London Grip*, *Magma*, *Modron*, *Natterlogue*, *Obsessed with Pipework*, Sídhe Press, *SINK*, *Spelt*, Spread the Word, *The Storms*, *Under the Radar*, and Verve Poetry Press

- the poets and mentors who have helped me grow: Caroline Bird, Rommi Smith, Kim Moore, Fióna Bolger, Katrina Moinet, and Sarah Pritchard, among many others

- Carola Luther, for allowing me to use a line from 'Architecture' for my golden shovel 'Alert'; Zo Copeland, for reading some of my manuscript and giving feedback, as well as being a lovely friend; and Stevie Ronnie for the kind words on 'Fainting' that have stayed with me

- my brilliant networks of writer friends across social media

- the organisations who have supported me and trusted me to write/perform/facilitate, including the Writing Squad, the Poetry Business, Rebecca Swift Foundation, Manchester Literature Festival, Portico Library, Islington Mill, Beatfreeks, Writerz and Scribez, Superbia, Oldham Coliseum, and Yorkshire Dance

- Manchester Poetry Library and Becky Swain and Martin Kratz for many lovely projects and providing such a magical and needed space

- Manchester and Tartu Cities of Literature for choosing 'Arrival' to appear in Estonian on Tartu buses, and translator Kersti Unt

- the Disabled Poets Prize for Highly Commending 'Could this be how to love?', a very affirming moment

- Lancaster Litfest for all their support over the years

- the fabulous open mics of Manchester and the North West: Blue Balloon's Poetry in the Park, Natter, Verbose, Words and Wellies, Queer as F*ck, Write Out Loud Sale, The Space Poetic, and many more

- Ó Bhéal in Cork for making me and my granma feel so welcome. It was a very special evening – enjoy the goose poem that came of it!

- Arts Council England for my 2021 Developing Your Creative Practice grant, and the Northern Writers Awards and Clare Pollard for my 2017 New North Poets Prize: moments of thinking, *I can do this*

- my parents, brother, cat, and all the extended family members who have been cheerleaders for my writing, with special shout-outs to my aunties Eibhlín and Fanchea, my granma Chris, and my cousin Christine, as well as to my auntie Etaín whose name inspired me to go on the mythology exploration that led to 'The fly house'

- Mr Wood, for first showing me how to love poetry through my love for nature

- my walking groups, for bringing me from the snows of Tintwistle to a rainy Hebden Bridge to walking barefoot to Hilbre Island

- my Irish traditional music group and the genius that is Michelle, for making me feel welcome and teaching me so much

- my friends and communities in Manchester and beyond. My quizzing and door-painting crew: Clare, Lucy, Michelle, and Rachel. Cass and dog Luis – a poem about Luis had to be cut from the collection due to formatting constraints, so I will declare here and now that he is the best boy. Ella, with a very cool boat

- Dan, for listening to me and helping me more than I can say, and, of course, having swagger

- the Indigo Girls for years of inspiration, with special thanks to Amy Ray, who I interviewed, for writing advice that has stuck with me

Finally, thank *you* for reading this. I aimed to write the poems that I always wanted to read, exploring queerness, chubbiness, periods, sensuality, neurodivergence, and animals – you can never have enough animals. I hope you enjoyed them. If things are really tough right now, please, try and stay. You have so much in you to give.